Work From Home Mastery

Proven Strategies to Earn a Full-Time Income

Without Leaving Your Houses

Evelyn Carter

1

Table of Contents

Chapter 1:How to Thrive in a Digital Economy

The remote work revolution has fundamentally transformed the way we approach employment, opening up unprecedented flexibility and opportunities for millions of people worldwide. This chapter examines the historical rise of remote work, the technologies that have enabled its success, and the myths and realities surrounding working from home in a digital economy.

History of Remote Work and Its Global Rise

Remote work isn't a new concept; however, it experienced exponential growth during the COVID-19 pandemic. Prior to 2020, remote work was often seen as a luxury, primarily for tech-savvy professionals or freelancers. Companies were hesitant to offer work-from-home arrangements, mainly due to concerns about productivity, accountability, and security.

The concept of telecommuting dates back to the 1970s when companies started experimenting with allowing employees to work remotely to reduce traffic congestion and pollution in urban areas. However, it was largely confined to specific industries like telecommunications and IT. The rise of high-speed internet, cloud computing, and collaborative tools in the early 2000s paved the way for broader adoption of remote work, but it was still limited in scope.

By 2020, the global pandemic forced a rapid acceleration in the adoption of remote work. Organizations were compelled to transition to work-from-home setups to maintain operations during lockdowns. This shift demonstrated that remote work is not only feasible but can also be productive and beneficial for both employees and employers. Surveys conducted after the pandemic revealed that many employees preferred the flexibility of remote work and that employers, too, saw cost savings and increased productivity.

Today, remote work is not only more widely accepted but is increasingly viewed as a permanent option for many companies. From startups to multinational corporations, businesses have embraced hybrid and fully remote models as part of their long-term workforce strategies.

Technologies Enabling Remote Work

Remote work's success is heavily reliant on advancements in technology, which have broken down traditional workplace barriers. Several key technologies have emerged as enablers of the digital workplace, making collaboration and communication easier, faster, and more secure.

1. **Cloud Computing**: The adoption of cloud computing has revolutionized remote work by allowing workers to access, store, and share data from anywhere with an internet connection. Cloud platforms like Google Drive, Dropbox, and Microsoft OneDrive offer seamless file-sharing capabilities, enabling team members to work on projects simultaneously without the constraints of geographical location.

2. **Video Conferencing Tools**: Platforms such as Zoom, Microsoft Teams, and Google Meet have become indispensable for remote work. These tools allow face-to-face communication, which helps maintain team cohesion, engagement, and collaboration. Video conferencing has replaced in-person meetings and even large-scale events, proving the

effectiveness of remote communication.

3. **Collaboration Software**: Tools like Slack, Trello, and Asana have optimized project management and team collaboration. These platforms provide shared workspaces, enabling teams to communicate in real time, assign tasks, and track project progress. Collaboration tools have made it possible to coordinate work across time zones and regions with minimal friction.

4. **Cybersecurity Solutions**: With the increase in remote work, cybersecurity has become a top priority for companies. VPNs (Virtual Private Networks), multi-factor authentication (MFA), and encrypted communication platforms ensure that sensitive company data is protected, even when accessed remotely. Cybersecurity

advancements have made it possible to maintain the same level of security in remote settings as in traditional offices.

Major Platforms and Industries Embracing Remote Work

Various industries have adapted to the remote work model, driven by technology and changing workforce dynamics. While remote work is particularly popular in the tech and creative sectors, other industries are also embracing the shift.

1. **Freelancing Platforms**: Websites like Upwork, Fiverr, and Freelancer have created marketplaces where skilled professionals can offer services ranging from graphic design to software development. These platforms allow workers to connect with clients globally and provide a steady stream of work without needing to be physically present in

an office. Freelancing has become a viable career option for millions of individuals seeking more control over their schedules.

2. **Tech and IT**: Companies in the tech industry, such as Microsoft, Google, and Salesforce, were some of the earliest adopters of remote work. The tech sector thrives on digital infrastructure, making it an ideal environment for remote teams. Even after pandemic-related lockdowns ended, many tech companies continued offering remote work or hybrid options.

3. **Customer Service and Support**: As remote work became more common, industries that traditionally required in-person interaction, such as customer service, adapted to the digital economy. Call centers and support roles are now frequently done remotely, aided by tools like

VoIP (Voice over Internet Protocol) and cloud-based customer service platforms.

4. **Education and Online Learning**: Remote work has expanded into the education sector as well. With platforms like Coursera, Udemy, and Khan Academy, educators and experts can deliver courses to a global audience. Online learning has not only become a supplement to traditional education but a thriving industry in its own right, creating work-from-home opportunities for instructors, course developers, and administrators.

Myths vs. Realities of Working from Home

Despite its rapid rise in popularity, there are several myths about remote work that persist. Let's debunk a few common misconceptions:

1. **Myth: Remote Workers Are Less Productive**

   Reality: Numerous studies have shown that remote workers can be more productive than their office-based counterparts. Without the distractions of a typical office environment—such as frequent meetings, interruptions, or commute-related stress—remote workers often accomplish more in less time. Additionally, remote workers tend to spend more time focused on deep work, contributing to higher-quality output.

2. **Myth: Remote Work Leads to Loneliness and Isolation**

   Reality: While working remotely can feel isolating for some, especially those who thrive on social interactions, it also offers flexibility to connect with colleagues and clients through video calls, chats, and collaborative tools. Many remote workers report improved work-life balance and greater control over their schedules, which can enhance overall well-being.

3. **Myth: Remote Work Is a Temporary Trend**
   Reality: Remote work is here to stay. While some companies may revert to office-based work, the demand for flexibility has made remote work a permanent fixture in many industries. Surveys show that employees now expect remote options, and businesses have adapted their operations accordingly.

4. **Myth: Remote Work Is Only for Tech Workers**
   Reality: While the tech industry was one of the first to embrace remote work, it is by no means the only sector doing so. Remote work

opportunities have expanded across industries like marketing, healthcare, finance, and education. The future of work is more flexible, with opportunities for workers of all backgrounds and industries.

The remote work revolution has fundamentally reshaped the landscape of employment in the digital economy. Through advancements in technology, a broad range of industries have embraced remote work, allowing millions of people to thrive outside of traditional office settings. As remote work continues to evolve, workers and businesses alike must adapt to the new realities of working from home, focusing on productivity, flexibility, and digital collaboration.

Chapter 2: Identifying Your Niche

When it comes to building a successful career in remote work, identifying your niche is one of the most critical steps. Your niche is the area where your unique skills, passions, and market demand intersect. By narrowing your focus and specializing in a specific market, you can distinguish yourself from the competition and create a profitable career path. This chapter guides you through understanding your strengths, assessing market demand, and finding a niche that is both fulfilling and profitable.

Understanding Your Unique Skills and How They Translate to Remote Work

The first step in finding your niche is gaining a clear understanding of your skills and passions. Many people approach remote work by focusing on broad categories like "freelancing" or "consulting," but success often lies in specialization. Before diving into potential markets, it's essential to reflect on what you're good at and what excites you. This will help you find a niche that resonates with your abilities and keeps you motivated.

1. **Self-Assessment**
   Start by asking yourself some key questions:

   - What skills have I developed throughout my career or personal experiences?

   - What tasks or projects do I excel at?

   - What type of work do I enjoy, and what are my passions outside of work?

To help guide this process, you can use the **SWOT analysis** technique, which stands for *Strengths*, *Weaknesses*, *Opportunities*, and *Threats*. This method allows you to map out your abilities and evaluate how they align with potential market opportunities.

2. **Skill Translation**

    Once you've assessed your strengths, consider how these skills translate to remote work. Some skills, such as writing, graphic design, and coding, are inherently suited for remote work, while others may require creative adaptation. For example:

    - A teacher can become an online tutor or course creator.

    - A project manager can pivot into virtual team management or freelance consulting.

    - A corporate trainer can create digital courses or webinars.

The key is to align your strengths with services that can be offered remotely.

Tools for Assessing Market Demand for Different Services or Products

Understanding your skills is only part of the equation. To build a successful business, you need to ensure there's demand for the services or products you plan to offer. Thankfully, there are several tools and techniques you can use to gauge market demand.

1. **Google Trends and Keyword Research**
   Google Trends allows you to track the popularity of specific search terms over time. You can input keywords related to your niche and see whether demand for these services is rising or falling. For example, searching for terms like "virtual assistant" or "content marketing" can show whether there's growing interest in these areas.

Keyword research tools like SEMrush, Ubersuggest, and Ahrefs can also give you insights into how often people are searching for certain services. High search volume indicates demand, while low competition suggests a potential opportunity for you to fill a gap in the market.

2. **Freelancing Platforms**
   Websites like Upwork, Fiverr, and Freelancer provide a wealth of information about what types of services are in demand. By browsing the categories, you can see which skills are most sought after by clients and how much freelancers are charging. This gives you a clearer idea of where opportunities lie and what pricing strategies you should adopt.

3. **Social Media and Online Communities**
   Platforms like LinkedIn, Facebook

groups, and Reddit communities can also be valuable resources for understanding market demand. By engaging in discussions and observing what people are asking for, you can identify emerging trends and potential niches. Online forums can also provide insights into common problems people face, which you can solve with your expertise.

4. **Industry Reports and Job Boards** Many industries release **annual reports** that provide insights into market growth and demand for specific roles. For example, fields like digital marketing and data analysis are projected to grow significantly in the coming years. Websites like Indeed and Glassdoor can also give you a sense of which jobs are frequently posted, indicating high demand.

Examples of Profitable Remote Niches in 2024

Now that we've covered how to assess market demand, let's look at some of the most profitable and growing remote niches for 2024.

1. **Content Writing and Copywriting**
   The demand for high-quality content continues to rise as businesses focus on digital marketing, SEO, and content-driven customer engagement. Content writers can specialize in blogs, articles, website copy, or technical writing. Copywriters, who focus on persuasive writing for marketing materials, landing pages, and advertisements, are also in high demand. Key sub-niches include:
   - SEO writing
   - Sales copywriting

- Technical writing
- Scriptwriting for podcasts and video content

2. **Virtual Assistance**

   Virtual assistants (VAs) provide administrative, technical, or creative support to businesses and entrepreneurs. As more companies embrace remote work, the need for VAs continues to grow. The role is versatile, and VAs can specialize in various tasks, such as:

   - Social media management
   - Email marketing and customer support
   - Bookkeeping and invoicing
   - Calendar and project management

To stand out in this niche, it helps to specialize in a particular industry, such as working exclusively with real estate agents, coaches, or small business owners.

3. **Digital Marketing**
   As businesses increasingly shift their focus to online marketing, digital marketers are in high demand. This niche offers several profitable subfields, including:

   - **Social Media Management**: Helping brands create and execute content strategies on platforms like Instagram, Facebook, and LinkedIn.

   - **SEO Specialist**: Improving website rankings on search engines through keyword optimization and content strategies.

   - **Paid Advertising Expert**: Running and managing ads on platforms like Google Ads,

Facebook Ads, and Instagram Ads.

- Email Marketing Specialist: Creating email campaigns to nurture customer relationships and increase sales.

4. **Graphic Design and Web Development**

The need for graphic designers and web developers continues to grow, especially as more businesses aim to improve their online presence. Remote designers work on projects ranging from website layouts and branding to social media graphics. Web developers can specialize in coding, user experience (UX) design, and app development. The rise of e-commerce has also increased demand for developers with expertise in platforms like Shopify and WooCommerce.

5. **Online Tutoring and Course Creation**
   With the global shift toward online learning, creating and teaching courses has become a lucrative niche. Platforms like Udemy, Teachable, and Skillshare allow you to create and sell online courses on almost any subject. Whether you're teaching academic subjects, professional skills, or personal development topics, there's a growing demand for online education.

6. **E-Commerce and Dropshipping**
   The rise of platforms like Shopify, Etsy, and Amazon has made it easier for entrepreneurs to start e-commerce businesses from home. Dropshipping, where you sell products directly from suppliers without holding inventory, is one of the most popular e-commerce

models. Niche markets in e-commerce, such as sustainable products, handmade goods, and personalized items, are thriving in 2024.

Practical Exercises: Evaluating Your Strengths and Market Opportunities

Now that you have a better understanding of how to find your niche, here are some practical exercises to help you evaluate your strengths and align them with market demand:

1. **Skills Inventory**
   Make a list of all your professional and personal skills. Include everything from technical abilities like coding and graphic design to soft skills like communication and problem-solving. Once you have your list, highlight the skills that excite you the most and consider

how they can be applied to remote work.

2. **Market Research**
   Using tools like Google Trends and keyword research, explore the market demand for services related to your skills. Create a list of potential niches that align with your strengths and research their growth potential.

3. **Competitor Analysis**
   Visit freelancing platforms like Upwork or Fiverr and look at top-rated freelancers in your chosen niche. What services are they offering? How are they pricing their services? By understanding the competitive landscape, you can find opportunities to differentiate yourself and carve out a unique space.

4. **Test Your Idea**

   If you're unsure about your niche, start by offering a small-scale service or product and testing the response. You could freelance part-time or create a digital product to gauge interest. Use feedback from clients and customers to refine your niche.

Identifying your niche is a crucial step in building a sustainable and fulfilling remote career. By aligning your unique skills with market demand, you can position yourself as an expert in a specific area and differentiate yourself from competitors. With the right approach and strategic planning, your niche can unlock both personal satisfaction and financial success in the growing digital economy.

Chapter 3: Creating the Perfect Work Environment for Productivity

Remote work offers flexibility, but achieving consistent productivity requires a well-structured home office environment. A successful remote worker must balance physical comfort, mental discipline, and effective time management. This chapter explores how to design an optimized workspace, implement time-blocking techniques, and maintain motivation while working from home, all of which are essential to sustaining long-term productivity.

Essential Equipment and Software for a Productive Home Office

The foundation of a productive work-from-home environment is the right combination of equipment and software that promotes efficiency and comfort.

Below are the essential components for a well-equipped home office.

1. **Ergonomic Furniture** Ergonomics is crucial for preventing discomfort and injury, especially when working long hours. Investing in a comfortable, ergonomic chair that supports your back and promotes proper posture can reduce the risk of strain and fatigue. A sit-stand desk is also beneficial, allowing you to alternate between sitting and standing throughout the day to improve circulation and reduce the risk of sedentary-related health issues.

Key Features of Ergonomic Furniture:

- Adjustable chair height and lumbar support
- Sit-stand desks for flexibility

- Anti-fatigue mats for standing workstations

- Proper desk setup that aligns monitor height with eye level to reduce neck strain

2. **Tech Essentials** A home office should be equipped with reliable technology to ensure smooth communication and workflow. A high-speed internet connection, a powerful computer, and a secondary monitor are all critical tools for productivity. A dual-monitor setup allows for more efficient multitasking, whether you're coding, writing, or designing.

Tech Must-Haves:

- High-speed, reliable internet connection

- A fast, efficient computer with adequate processing power for your tasks

- External monitors for enhanced multitasking and a better overview of projects

- Noise-cancelling headphones for focusing in a noisy environment

3. **Software for Collaboration and Efficiency** The right software can streamline workflows and enhance collaboration, even when working remotely. Project management tools like Trello, Asana, or Monday.com help track tasks, while communication platforms like Slack and Microsoft Teams foster real-time interaction. Additionally, cloud-based services such as Google Workspace or Microsoft OneDrive ensure easy access to documents,

enabling seamless collaboration with clients or colleagues.

Software Essentials:

- o Project management tools (e.g., Trello, Asana, Monday.com)

- o Communication tools (e.g., Slack, Zoom, Microsoft Teams)

- o Cloud storage for document sharing (e.g., Google Drive, Dropbox)

- o Time-tracking apps (e.g., Toggl, Clockify) to monitor work hours

Time-Blocking Techniques and Work-Life Balance

One of the biggest challenges remote workers face is managing their time effectively while maintaining a healthy work-life balance. Time-blocking, a productivity technique that involves scheduling specific blocks of time for different tasks, can help create structure and ensure that important tasks get completed efficiently.

1. **How Time-Blocking Works** Time-blocking is the practice of allocating specific periods in your day to focus on particular tasks. Instead of multitasking, which can lead to scattered attention and decreased productivity, time-blocking encourages deep work during set intervals. For example, you might dedicate the first hour of your day to answering emails, followed by a three-hour block for high-priority projects.

Steps for Effective Time-Blocking:

- o Divide your day into chunks of time, each designated for a specific task or type of work.

- Prioritize tasks by importance and urgency, ensuring that the most critical work is done when you're most alert.

- Include breaks and time for personal activities to avoid burnout.

- Review and adjust your time blocks weekly to ensure they're aligned with your goals.

2. **Maintaining Work-Life Balance**
   One risk of working from home is the blurring of boundaries between personal life and work. Without the clear separation that a physical office provides, it's easy to fall into the trap of overworking or becoming distracted by household responsibilities.

To maintain work-life balance, it's essential to establish routines and create clear distinctions between work time and personal time. Set consistent working hours and avoid the temptation to check emails or continue working outside of these times. Designating a specific area in your home for work—whether it's a separate room or a corner of your living space—can also help create a psychological boundary between work and leisure.

Work-Life Balance Tips:

- Set defined working hours and stick to them as much as possible.

- Create a morning routine that signals the start of your workday (e.g., changing into work clothes, setting up your workspace).

- Take regular breaks, ideally away from your workspace, to recharge.

- o Establish a clear end-of-day routine to disconnect from work (e.g., shutting down your computer, going for a walk).

Strategies for Staying Motivated and Avoiding Burnout

Working from home requires a higher level of self-discipline and intrinsic motivation. Without the immediate presence of supervisors or coworkers, it's easy to lose focus, procrastinate, or experience burnout. Here are strategies to maintain motivation and prevent fatigue while working remotely.

1. **Having well-defined objectives ensures clarity and focus. To stay on track, divide major projects into smaller, actionable steps, each with its own specific deadline. This approach not only simplifies complex tasks but also boosts productivity by making**

progress more achievable.. This creates a sense of progress and achievement, which can be incredibly motivating. Additionally, setting both short-term and long-term goals can help you stay focused and aligned with your broader career objectives.

Goal-Setting Tips:

- Use the SMART method (Specific, Measurable, Achievable, Relevant, Time-bound) to set clear goals.

- Break down larger projects into daily or weekly tasks.

- Track progress regularly and celebrate small wins to maintain momentum.

2. **Use the Pomodoro Technique for Focus** The Pomodoro Technique is a time management method that

encourages short bursts of focused work followed by brief breaks. This approach helps maintain high levels of concentration while avoiding mental fatigue. To use the Pomodoro Technique, work for 25 minutes, take a five-minute break, and repeat the cycle four times before taking a longer break.

Pomodoro Technique Steps:

- o Choose a task and set a timer for 25 minutes.

- o Work uninterrupted for the duration of the timer.

- o Take a five-minute break when the timer goes off.

- o Aftcr four "Pomodoros," take a longer 15-30 minute break.

3. **Avoiding Burnout** Remote work can blur the lines between work and personal time, leading to extended

hours and eventual burnout. To avoid this, prioritize self-care and regularly check in with your mental and physical health. Make sure to incorporate activities that help you unwind, whether that's exercising, reading, or spending time with family and friends.

Burnout Prevention Tips:

- o Schedule regular breaks and time away from screens.

- o Create a work environment that allows for occasional movement, such as standing desks or walking breaks.

- o Set clear boundaries between work and relaxation, avoiding work tasks during personal time.

- o Reach out to colleagues or friends for social interaction to combat isolation.

Creating the perfect work environment for productivity goes beyond simply having the right equipment. It requires intentional design, time management techniques like time-blocking, and mental discipline to maintain motivation and avoid burnout. By implementing these strategies, remote workers can not only increase their productivity but also enjoy a balanced, fulfilling work-from-home lifestyle.

Chapter 4: Monetizing Your Skills –

Turn Your Passion into Profit

In today's rapidly evolving digital economy, turning your skills and passions into a profitable income stream is not only possible but increasingly achievable. Whether you're aiming to freelance, consult, or create digital products, leveraging your existing abilities is the foundation for building a successful business. This chapter will guide you through the process of converting your skills into an income, setting competitive rates, building an online portfolio, and eventually scaling your freelance work into a full-time business.

How to Convert Existing Skills into an Income Stream

To start generating income from your skills, it's essential to first identify what you excel at and how those skills can translate into marketable services. Almost any skill—from writing, design, and programming to photography, tutoring, and crafting—can be monetized in today's digital landscape.

1. **Skill Identification and Specialization** The first step is to clearly define your strengths. Make a list of the skills you've acquired through education, work experience, or even hobbies. Then, focus on how these skills can solve problems for others. For example:

   o A **graphic designer** can create logos, branding materials, and websites.

   o A **writer** can offer content writing, copywriting, or technical writing services.

- A **teacher** can become an online tutor or create digital courses.

Once you've identified your skill set, consider specializing in a niche market. Specialization allows you to stand out from the competition by offering highly tailored services. For instance, if you are a graphic designer, narrowing your focus to "branding for eco-friendly companies" can help you attract a specific audience.

2. **Freelancing Platforms** Freelancing platforms such as Upwork, Fiverr, and Freelancer provide excellent starting points for monetizing your skills. These platforms connect freelancers with clients looking for specific services. You can create a profile showcasing your abilities, submit proposals for projects, and build a reputation based on reviews.

Additionally, platforms like LinkedIn can be valuable for finding freelance opportunities. LinkedIn's job boards and professional networking features make it a great place to connect with potential clients and showcase your skills.

3. **Consulting Services** If you have advanced knowledge or experience in a particular field, offering consulting services can be a lucrative option. Consultants provide expertise and strategic advice to businesses or individuals looking to improve their operations, marketing, or management processes. Consultants often charge higher rates than freelancers due to the specialized nature of their services.

4. **Creating Digital Products** If you prefer to create passive income streams, consider packaging your knowledge into digital products. E-books, online courses, templates,

and guides are all examples of digital products that can generate income over time. Platforms like Udemy, Teachable, and Etsy make it easy to sell these products globally. Digital products require upfront work to create, but they can continue to generate income with minimal ongoing effort.

Setting Rates: Understanding the Value of Your Work and How to Negotiate

One of the most challenging aspects of freelancing or consulting is determining how much to charge for your services. Pricing is a delicate balance—you want to ensure that you are being fairly compensated for your time and expertise, while also remaining competitive in the marketplace.

1. **Hourly vs. Project-Based Rates**
   There are two main ways to charge

for freelance services: hourly rates or project-based fees.

- o **Hourly rates** are common for services where the time required to complete a task may vary, such as consulting, graphic design, or writing.

- o **Project-based fees** are often more appealing to clients because they offer a set cost for a particular deliverable, such as a completed website, a logo design, or a specific number of blog posts.

To determine your rates, consider:

- o The level of expertise required.

- o The complexity of the project.

- o The value it brings to the client.

o Your expenses (software, taxes, etc.).

2. **Researching Market Rates** It's important to research industry standards and competitive rates for your niche. Freelance platforms, job boards, and industry associations often publish rate guidelines. For example:

   o Writers can charge between $0.10 and $2.00 per word, depending on their experience and the complexity of the project.

   o Web designers may charge anywhere from $25 to $150 per hour, depending on their skill level and the complexity of the project.

Keep in mind that rates can vary depending on geographic location, the client's budget, and the urgency of the work.

3. **Negotiating with Clients** When negotiating rates with clients, be transparent about the value you bring. Highlight your experience, past successes, and how your work can help them achieve their goals. Be prepared to justify your rates and, if necessary, negotiate in terms of project scope rather than lowering your fees. For instance, if a client has a limited budget, you can offer to scale back the deliverables rather than reduce your rate.

Building an Online Portfolio and Reputation

A professional online portfolio is essential for showcasing your skills, previous work, and expertise to potential clients. Your portfolio is often the first impression clients will have of you, so it's crucial to present yourself in the best light.

1. **Portfolio Website** Creating a dedicated website for your freelance business allows you to highlight your services, share testimonials, and provide examples of your work. Some elements to include in your portfolio are:

   o **Service Offerings**: Clearly describe what services you offer, such as content writing, web development, or consulting.

   o **Work Samples**: Showcase completed projects or case studies that demonstrate your skills. If you're just starting and don't have many examples, consider creating sample work or offering a few discounted projects in exchange for testimonials.

- o **Client Testimonials**: Positive reviews from satisfied clients build credibility and trust with new clients.

- o **Contact Information**: Make it easy for potential clients to reach you by including a contact form or direct email.

2. **Utilizing Social Media** In addition to your portfolio website, social media platforms can be effective tools for building your reputation. LinkedIn, Instagram, and Twitter are ideal for sharing your expertise and promoting your work. By regularly posting content related to your niche, such as tips, blog posts, or case studies, you can attract followers who may turn into clients.

3. **Gaining Reviews and Testimonials**
   Client reviews and testimonials are incredibly valuable for establishing trust and credibility. After completing a project, ask your clients to leave a review or provide a testimonial that you can showcase on your website or social media profiles. Positive feedback is one of the most effective ways to build your reputation and secure future business.

Steps to Scale from Freelancer to Business Owner

While freelancing is an excellent way to start monetizing your skills, many professionals aspire to grow their freelance work into a full-fledged business. Scaling your work involves increasing your client base, expanding your service offerings, and potentially hiring additional team members.

1. **Automating Processes** As your workload grows, automating repetitive tasks can free up your time to focus on high-value activities. Tools like **Calendly** can automate scheduling, while **QuickBooks** or **FreshBooks** can handle invoicing and accounting. Using a project management tool like **Trello** or **Asana** can help you keep track of ongoing projects and deadlines.

2. **Expanding Your Services** As you gain more experience, consider expanding your service offerings. For example, a freelance web designer could start offering SEO optimization or digital marketing services. By diversifying your services, you can attract more clients and increase your revenue streams.

3. **Building a Team** To scale your business further, you may need to

hire subcontractors or employees to assist with tasks that you either don't have the time for or aren't within your area of expertise. You can hire virtual assistants, other freelancers, or even bring on full-time staff to handle client communications, marketing, and administrative tasks.

4. **Developing Passive Income Streams** Once you've established a solid client base, you can begin building passive income streams to supplement your freelance work. Creating digital products, such as e-books, courses, or templates, can generate income without requiring active time investment. Additionally, affiliate marketing and creating membership sites or subscription-based services can provide consistent income with minimal ongoing effort.

Turning your skills and passions into a profitable business is a rewarding path that requires strategy, persistence, and continuous learning. By understanding your market, setting the right prices, building a strong online presence, and scaling your efforts, you can transform your freelance work into a sustainable, thriving business. As you grow, automation, expanded services, and passive income streams will allow you to achieve greater financial independence and work-life balance.

Chapter 5: Building Multiple Income Streams

In today's digital age, relying on a single source of income can be risky, especially for remote workers or freelancers. Diversifying your income through multiple streams not only provides financial security but also helps you build a sustainable and scalable business. This chapter explores the concept of passive income, outlines step-by-step strategies to start blogs, YouTube channels, or podcasts, and offers insights into affiliate marketing and creating digital products such as online courses, e-books, and templates.

Introduction to Passive Income: What It Is and How to Build It

Passive income refers to money earned with minimal active effort after the initial work is done. Unlike a traditional job where income is tied to hours worked, passive income continues to generate earnings even when you're not actively working on it. While passive income may require upfront time, resources, and investment, it can become a sustainable revenue source over time.

Types of Passive Income:

1. **Blogging and Affiliate Marketing**: Writing content that generates traffic and earns income through ads or affiliate commissions.

2. **Online Courses**: Creating a course that provides value to learners, sold on platforms like Udemy or Teachable.

3. **Digital Products**: E-books, templates, or tools that offer solutions to problems people face and can be sold repeatedly without additional effort.

4. **Investments**: Generating income from financial investments such as stocks, bonds, or real estate.

Step-by-Step Guide to Starting a Blog, YouTube Channel, or Podcast

One of the most effective ways to build passive income is by creating content that attracts a consistent audience. Blogs, YouTube channels, and podcasts offer scalable platforms to share knowledge, build a brand, and generate revenue through ads, sponsorships, and affiliate marketing.

1. **Starting a Blog** Blogging remains one of the most accessible ways to build passive income. It allows you to share expertise, build an audience, and monetize through advertising, sponsored posts, and affiliate marketing.

Step-by-Step Process:

- **Choose a Niche**: Pick a topic that aligns with your passion and skills, such as personal finance, fitness, or travel.

- **Set Up a Website**: Use platforms like WordPress or Wix to build your blog. You'll need a domain name, hosting provider, and a website theme.

- **Create Valuable Content**: Focus on creating content that addresses the needs and questions of your target audience. Write blog posts that offer solutions to problems or provide insightful guides.

- **Monetize the Blog**: Once you have consistent traffic, you can monetize through Google AdSense, affiliate marketing, sponsored content, or selling your own products.

2. **Starting a YouTube Channel** Video content is increasingly popular, and YouTube provides a great platform to reach a large audience while earning ad revenue.

Step-by-Step Process:

- o **Choose a Niche**: Just like blogging, your channel needs to focus on a specific area, whether it's tech tutorials, cooking, or fitness.

- o **Create Quality Content**: Invest in good lighting, sound, and video editing tools to make your content visually appealing. Focus on solving problems or providing entertainment in your niche.

- o **Optimize for SEO**: Use keywords in your video titles, descriptions, and tags to help your content rank higher on YouTube.

- o **Monetize with Ads and Sponsorships**: Once you meet YouTube's Partner Program requirements (1,000 subscribers and 4,000 watch hours), you can start earning ad revenue. Additionally, as your audience grows, brands may approach you for sponsorship opportunities.

3. **Starting a Podcast** Podcasting has become a popular medium for sharing long-form content and building authority in a particular niche. With the right strategy, podcasts can generate revenue through sponsorships, listener donations, or product sales.

Step-by-Step Process:

o **Choose a Niche and Format**: Decide on the podcast's theme and format, whether it's interview-based, solo episodes, or panel discussions.

o **Invest in Equipment**: While podcasts don't require video, high-quality audio is essential. Invest in a good microphone and audio editing software.

o **Publish Consistently**: Just like with blogs and YouTube channels, consistency is key. Develop a content calendar and stick to a schedule.

o **Monetize with Sponsorships and Ads**: As your podcast gains listeners, you can monetize through ads, sponsorships, or even premium content for subscribers.

Affiliate Marketing Strategies That Work in 2024

Affiliate marketing is a powerful way to generate passive income by promoting other people's products and earning commissions for every sale made through your unique referral links. Here are strategies for making affiliate marketing work in 2024.

1. **Choose the Right Products and Niche** Select products or services that align with your audience's needs. Whether you're blogging, running a YouTube channel, or podcasting, your audience will trust your recommendations if they are relevant and valuable.

2. **Join Reliable Affiliate Programs** Platforms like **Amazon Associates**, **ShareASale**, and **CJ Affiliate** offer access to thousands of products in different niches. Research the

commission structures, payout methods, and product quality before joining a program.

3. **Create Honest and In-Depth Reviews** Transparency and trust are critical in affiliate marketing. Write or record in-depth reviews of the products you are promoting, explaining their benefits, drawbacks, and practical uses. Avoid over-promoting or recommending products you don't believe in, as it could damage your reputation.

4. **Utilize SEO and Social Media** Incorporate search engine optimization (SEO) strategies to drive organic traffic to your blog or YouTube channel. Social media platforms such as Instagram, Twitter, and Pinterest can also be powerful tools for sharing affiliate links, increasing visibility, and driving conversions.

5. **Track Your Performance** Use tools like **Google Analytics** or affiliate program dashboards to monitor the performance of your affiliate links. Understanding what products are selling well and where your traffic is coming from will help you refine your strategies over time.

Creating and Selling Online Courses or Digital Products

One of the most lucrative ways to generate passive income is by creating and selling digital products such as online courses, e-books, or templates. These products offer value to customers and can be sold repeatedly with little to no additional effort.

1. **Creating Online Courses** If you have expertise in a particular subject, you can create an online course to teach others. Platforms like **Udemy**, **Teachable**, and

Skillshare make it easy to create and sell courses on various topics, from photography to programming.

Steps to Create a Course:

- o **Choose a Topic**: Focus on a subject you're knowledgeable about and that people are willing to pay to learn. This could be anything from language learning to business skills.

- o **Develop Course Content**: Structure your course into lessons or modules. Use video, slides, quizzes, and downloadable resources to keep learners engaged.

- o **Upload to a Platform**: After creating the content, upload it to a course platform. Set a price based on the course's value and market demand.

- **Market Your Course**: Promote your course through social media, email newsletters, and partnerships to attract students.

2. **Selling E-Books and Templates** E-books and templates are great digital products that can be created once and sold multiple times. Whether you're writing a how-to guide, offering photography presets, or designing business templates, these products offer value and convenience to your audience.

Steps to Create Digital Products:

- **Identify Your Audience**: Who are you creating the product for? What problem does it solve? Knowing your target audience will help you tailor the product to meet their needs.

67

- **Create the Product**: Whether it's an e-book or a template, ensure that it's high-quality, professional, and easy to use.

- **Sell Through Online Marketplaces**: Platforms like **Etsy**, **Gumroad**, and **Amazon Kindle Direct Publishing (KDP)** allow you to sell digital products to a global audience.

- **Promote on Multiple Channels**: Use social media, email marketing, and SEO to drive traffic to your product listings.

Building multiple income streams is essential for creating long-term financial stability and independence. Whether you're starting a blog, creating digital products, or engaging in affiliate marketing, the key to success lies in consistency, creativity, and delivering value to your audience. By diversifying your income streams and leveraging the vast opportunities in the digital space, you can build a sustainable and scalable business that generates income even when you're not actively working.

Chapter 6: Marketing Yourself Online –

The Power of Personal Branding

In today's highly competitive digital marketplace, establishing a personal brand is crucial for anyone looking to stand out and attract clients or customers. A strong personal brand communicates your value, expertise, and unique qualities to potential clients or employers. This chapter will guide you through the steps of developing a personal brand, building a professional online presence, and effectively marketing yourself through content, SEO, and networking.

Developing a Personal Brand in Today's Digital World

Your personal brand is the perception others have of you based on the content you create, your online interactions, and your professional reputation. In an era where much of your professional and personal life is on display online, carefully crafting your personal brand is key to success.

1. **Why Personal Branding Matters** Personal branding helps you position yourself as an expert in your field. Whether you're a freelancer, consultant, or business owner, your personal brand can attract opportunities that align with your goals and skills. A strong brand helps you differentiate yourself from competitors and build trust with potential clients or employers.

2. **Defining Your Brand** The first step in developing a personal brand is self-reflection. Consider your values, skills, and what makes you unique. Ask yourself:

   - What are my strengths and expertise?

- What kind of clients or audience do I want to attract?

- What values and messages do I want to communicate through my brand?

Your personal brand should reflect your authentic self and align with your long-term goals. For example, if you're a marketing consultant specializing in helping small businesses, your brand should convey expertise in marketing strategy while also demonstrating an understanding of the unique challenges faced by small businesses.

Building a Professional Website and Social Media Profiles

Having an online presence is essential for personal branding. A professional website and active social media profiles serve as your digital resume, showcasing your skills, portfolio, and personality. Here's how to get started.

1. **Creating a Professional Website**
Your website is the cornerstone of your online presence. It's where potential clients or employers will go to learn more about you, your services, and your expertise. Here's what to include on your website:

   - **About Me/Services Page**: Clearly explain who you are and what services or value you offer. Include your background, expertise, and achievements.

   - **Portfolio**: Showcase your work or projects you've completed. Whether you're a writer, designer, or consultant, having a portfolio helps potential clients assess your skills and capabilities.

   - **Testimonials**: Add reviews or testimonials from past clients or employers to build trust and credibility.

○ **Blog**: If you have expertise to share, a blog is an excellent way to demonstrate your knowledge, improve your site's SEO, and attract clients.

For those with limited web development experience, platforms like WordPress, Wix, and Squarespace offer user-friendly templates that allow you to build a professional website without needing extensive technical skills.

2. **Optimizing Your Social Media Profiles** Social media is a powerful tool for personal branding. It's where you can showcase your personality, interact with others, and promote your work. Here are some key platforms to consider:

○ **LinkedIn**: A must-have for professionals, LinkedIn allows you to connect with others in your industry, showcase your experience, and share thought leadership content. Optimize your profile by including a professional photo, a detailed bio, and your work history.

- o **Instagram**: If your work is visually driven (like photography, design, or fashion), Instagram is a great platform for showcasing your portfolio.

- o **Twitter**: Twitter is a great platform for engaging in industry conversations, sharing content, and building a network.

- o **YouTube or TikTok**: If video is part of your personal brand, platforms like YouTube or TikTok can help you create engaging, educational content that resonates with your audience.

Content Marketing: Blogging, Social Media, and SEO Strategies

Content marketing plays a crucial role in establishing your personal brand by showcasing your expertise and providing value to your audience. By producing consistent, high-quality content, you can drive traffic to your website, build relationships with your audience, and increase your visibility online.

1. **Blogging as a Branding Tool**
   Blogging allows you to share your knowledge, opinions, and insights on topics relevant to your niche. Not only does this position you as a thought leader, but it also improves your website's SEO (search engine optimization), making it easier for

potential clients to find you. Here's how to start:

- o **Choose Relevant Topics**: Write about topics that are related to your expertise and that your target audience is interested in. For example, if you're a financial advisor, you could write about investment strategies, financial planning tips, or market trends.

- o **Optimize for SEO**: Research keywords that your audience is searching for and include them in your blog posts. This helps improve your ranking on search engines like Google.

- o **Promote Your Blog**: Share your blog posts on social media, in email newsletters, and on relevant online forums to increase visibility.

2. **Using Social Media for Content Marketing** Social media platforms are perfect for distributing content and engaging with your audience. Here are some strategies:

   o **Post Consistently**: Develop a content calendar and post regularly to keep your audience engaged. This could include sharing blog posts, behind-the-scenes content, or educational videos.

   o **Engage with Your Audience**: Respond to comments and messages from your followers. Building relationships with your audience helps establish trust and loyalty.

   o **Leverage Hashtags**: Use relevant hashtags to increase the reach of your posts and attract a broader audience. For example, if you're a web developer, you could use hashtags like #WebDevelopment or #TechTips.

3. **SEO Strategies to Increase Your Online Presence** SEO is essential for increasing the visibility of your personal brand online. By optimizing your website and content for search engines, you can attract more traffic and potential clients. Some key SEO strategies include:

   o **Keyword Research**: Identify the search terms your audience is using and include them in your website's content, blog posts, and meta descriptions.

   o **Quality Content**: Search engines prioritize websites that offer high-quality, informative content. Regularly updating your blog or website with fresh, valuable content can improve your ranking.

- o **Link Building**: Building backlinks (links from other websites to yours) is crucial for improving SEO. Reach out to industry blogs or websites for guest posting opportunities to build your backlink profile.

How to Network and Find Clients Online

Once you've established a strong personal brand, the next step is to actively network and find clients or customers. The internet provides countless opportunities to connect with potential clients, collaborators, and employers.

1. **Leveraging LinkedIn** LinkedIn is a powerful networking tool for professionals. To network effectively on LinkedIn:

- **Connect with Industry Professionals**: Reach out to people in your industry, introduce yourself, and establish connections. Don't just send generic connection requests; personalize your message and explain why you'd like to connect.

- **Engage with Content**: Comment on posts, join discussions, and share content to increase your visibility in the LinkedIn community.

- **Join LinkedIn Groups**: Participating in LinkedIn Groups relevant to your industry allows you to connect with like-minded professionals, share your expertise, and build relationships with potential clients.

2. **Join Online Communities and Forums** Industry-specific forums, Facebook groups, and online communities offer great opportunities to network and find clients. By participating in discussions, offering advice, and sharing your knowledge, you can establish yourself as an expert in your field. Websites like Reddit and Quora also provide platforms to answer questions and showcase your expertise.

3. **Attend Virtual Events and Webinars** Virtual conferences, webinars, and networking events allow you to connect with professionals in your field and grow your network from the comfort of your home. These events often have live chats or breakout rooms where you can introduce yourself to other attendees and share your expertise.

4. **Offer Free Value to Build Relationships** Offering free advice, templates, or resources can be an excellent way to build relationships with potential clients. For example, you could offer a free consultation or create a downloadable guide that addresses common pain points your target audience faces. By providing value upfront, you increase the chances of turning prospects into paying clients.

Personal branding is a powerful tool in today's digital economy, allowing you to stand out, build credibility, and attract the clients or customers you want. By developing a personal brand, building a strong online presence, producing valuable content, and networking effectively, you can establish yourself as a leader in your field. With the right strategy and consistent effort, your personal brand can become your most valuable asset, opening doors to new opportunities and lasting professional success.

Chapter 7: Mastering the Art of Time Management

Time management is one of the most critical skills for remote workers to master. Without the structure of a traditional office environment, working from home can lead to distractions, procrastination, or even burnout from overworking. In this chapter, we will explore practical time management strategies, including proven techniques like the Pomodoro Technique and the Eisenhower Matrix, and review tools such as Trello and Asana that help you stay organized and productive. We'll also discuss how to establish work-life boundaries to maintain a healthy and balanced routine while working remotely.

Essential Time Management Techniques for Remote Workers

Effective time management is about more than just organizing your to-do list. It involves understanding your priorities, breaking tasks into manageable segments, and maintaining focus. Here are a few widely adopted time management techniques that can help you achieve optimal productivity.

1. **The Pomodoro Technique** The Pomodoro Technique is a time management method that breaks your work into intervals, traditionally 25 minutes long, followed by a 5-minute break. After four consecutive "Pomodoros," you take a longer break, typically 15–30 minutes. This technique helps you maintain intense focus for short bursts, preventing burnout and improving productivity.

How it works:

   o Choose a task to focus on.

   o Set a timer for 25 minutes and work uninterrupted.

- o Take a 5-minute break when the timer goes off.

Benefits:

- o Encourages deep work by limiting distractions.

- o Breaks tasks into manageable intervals, making large projects feel less overwhelming.

- o Reduces mental fatigue by incorporating regular breaks.

2. **The Eisenhower Matrix** The Eisenhower Matrix, also known as the Urgent-Important Matrix, helps you prioritize tasks by categorizing them into four quadrants based on their urgency and importance. This method helps you focus on what truly matters, minimizing the time spent on unimportant tasks.

The four quadrants:

- Urgent and Important: Tasks that require immediate attention and have significant consequences, like deadlines or emergencies.

- Important but Not Urgent: Tasks that contribute to long-term goals but don't need immediate action, such as strategic planning or skill development.

- Urgent but Not Important: Tasks that require attention but don't significantly impact your goals, like some meetings or phone calls.

- Not Urgent and Not Important: Tasks that are essentially time-wasters, such as excessive social media browsing or irrelevant tasks.

How to use it:

- Categorize your tasks into one of the four quadrants.

- Focus on tasks in the **Urgent and Important** quadrant first.

- Delegate or defer tasks in the **Urgent but Not Important** quadrant.

- Avoid tasks in the **Not Urgent and Not Important** quadrant.

Benefits:

- Helps prioritize tasks that align with long-term goals.

- Reduces time spent on non-essential activities.

- Provides clarity on what needs immediate attention.

3. **Time Blocking** Time blocking involves scheduling specific blocks of time for particular tasks or activities. By dedicating time to high-

priority tasks, you ensure that they get the focus and attention they deserve without being overshadowed by distractions.

How it works:

- Break your day into time blocks dedicated to specific tasks or categories of work (e.g., "email management" from 9:00–9:30, "content creation" from 10:00–12:00).

- Stick to these time slots as closely as possible.

- Adjust your time blocks weekly based on productivity patterns and workload.

Benefits:

- Enhances focus on single tasks by eliminating multitasking.

- Encourages disciplined time management and structure.

- o Ensures that essential tasks don't fall through the cracks.

Productivity Tools and Apps to Keep Your Projects Organized

Remote work often requires juggling multiple projects and deadlines. To manage this complexity, leveraging project management and productivity tools can make a significant difference in your effectiveness.

1. **Trello** Trello is a visual project management tool that uses boards, lists, and cards to organize tasks. It's perfect for tracking individual tasks, group projects, or long-term goals.

How to use Trello:

- o Create a board for each project or area of your work.

- o Add lists to represent different stages of the project (e.g., "To-

Do," "In Progress," and "Completed").

- o Create cards for individual tasks and move them across lists as you progress.

Benefits:

- o Offers a simple, intuitive visual representation of your projects.

- o Enables easy collaboration with teams through shared boards.

- o Integrates with other tools like Google Drive and Slack for seamless workflow management.

2. **Asana** Asana is another powerful project management tool that helps teams and individuals organize tasks, set deadlines, and track progress. Unlike Trello's visual

interface, Asana offers more detailed project tracking, with features for task dependencies, subtasks, and project overviews.

How to use Asana:

- Set up projects for your tasks or long-term goals.

- Break larger tasks into subtasks and assign deadlines.

- Use the timeline view to map out projects over time.

Benefits:

- Offers advanced features like task dependencies and automation.

- Ideal for both individual users and collaborative team environments.

- Provides a comprehensive overview of project timelines and priorities.

3. **Todoist** Todoist is a popular task management tool designed to keep your to-do lists organized. Its simplicity and ease of use make it an excellent choice for remote workers managing daily tasks.

How to use Todoist:

- Create projects to categorize your tasks (e.g., "Work," "Personal," or "Freelance Clients").

- Set deadlines and prioritize tasks using the "Priority" feature.

- Track progress and celebrate completed tasks with the built-in productivity tracking.

Benefits:

- Simple and user-friendly, ideal for daily task management.

- Integrates with apps like Google Calendar and Slack for smooth scheduling.

- Tracks productivity and helps with time management.

4. **Google Calendar** Google Calendar remains one of the most versatile tools for managing time and scheduling. Use it to set reminders, block out time for focused work, and sync your calendar with other tools.

How to use Google Calendar:

- Block off time for essential tasks, meetings, and breaks.

- Use color-coded labels to differentiate between various types of work.

- Set reminders for deadlines or important events.

Benefits:

- o Easily syncs across devices, ensuring you never miss a meeting or task.

- o Ideal for scheduling and time blocking.

- o Integrates with project management tools and email apps for seamless coordination.

How to Manage Work-Life Boundaries in a Home Setting

One of the greatest challenges for remote workers is maintaining a clear distinction between work and personal life. Without the physical separation of an office, work can easily bleed into personal time, leading to stress, burnout, and reduced productivity.

1. **Create a Designated Workspace**
   One of the most effective ways to

establish work-life boundaries is by creating a designated workspace in your home. This could be a home office or even a small desk in the corner of a room. The key is to ensure that this space is used exclusively for work.

Benefits:

- ○ Helps you mentally shift into "work mode" when you sit at your desk.

- ○ Reduces distractions and interruptions from personal life.

- ○ Allows for a clear boundary between your workspace and relaxation areas.

2. **Set Clear Working Hours** Establish set working hours and communicate these to your family, housemates, or anyone who might interrupt you.

Once your workday is over, resist the temptation to continue working or check emails.

Tips:

- o Use your calendar to block off specific work hours.

- o Set alarms or reminders to start and end your workday.

- o Communicate your work schedule to anyone sharing your space.

3. **Take Breaks and Maintain Downtime** Incorporating regular breaks throughout the day is essential for maintaining mental health and productivity. Use techniques like Pomodoro to schedule breaks, or step outside for a quick walk to recharge. Downtime is equally important, so make sure to disconnect from work entirely

during weekends or after work hours.

Benefits:

- Reduces burnout and helps you stay focused when working.

- Encourages better work-life balance and mental well-being.

- Improves creativity and problem-solving through mental rest.

4. **Establish a Work Shut-Down Routine** At the end of the day, create a routine that signals the end of work. This could involve tidying up your workspace, reviewing your to-do list for the next day, or physically leaving your home office. Having a clear shut-down routine helps you mentally disconnect from work,

making it easier to transition into personal time.

Effectively managing your time is essential for excelling in a remote work setting.. By incorporating techniques like the Pomodoro Technique and Eisenhower Matrix, and using tools like Trello and Asana, remote workers can stay organized, focused, and productive. Equally important is managing work-life boundaries to avoid burnout and maintain a healthy balance between professional and personal life. When applied consistently, these strategies will help you maximize your efficiency and make the most of your time while working from home.

Chapter 8: Scaling Your Remote Business – From Solo to CEO

Scaling a remote business is both an exciting and challenging endeavor. As a solo entrepreneur or freelancer, you've laid the groundwork, honed your skills, and developed a client base. Now, it's time to take your business to the next level by expanding your team, increasing your efficiency, and embracing automation. This chapter will guide you through the process of scaling your business without compromising on quality, hiring and managing a remote team, and leveraging automation to optimize workflows. We'll also examine case studies of entrepreneurs who successfully transitioned from solopreneurs to CEOs.

How to Scale Your Business Without Losing Quality

One of the biggest challenges in scaling a business is maintaining the high standards of quality that attracted your initial clients while expanding operations. As you scale, you'll need to focus on consistency, systems, and processes that allow you to manage growth without sacrificing excellence.

1. **Establish Clear Processes** The key to scaling a business is systematizing your work. Start by documenting the core processes you use to deliver services to your clients. This could be anything from how you onboard new clients to the steps you take to complete projects. Documenting these processes ensures that as you grow, your team can follow the same guidelines and deliver consistent results.

Steps to create processes:

- Define Key Tasks: Break down your services into individual tasks. For example, if you're a freelance writer, this might include research, drafting, revisions, and final submissions.

- Create Standard Operating Procedures (SOPs): SOPs are step-by-step instructions that outline how to perform tasks within your business. They help ensure consistency, especially when you delegate work to others.

- Utilize Project Management Tools: Tools like Asana, Monday.com, or Trello can help you manage workflows, track progress, and ensure that tasks are completed on time.

103

2. **Focus on Your Core Strengths** As you scale, it's important to focus on the core services or products that made your business successful. Trying to expand into too many areas at once can dilute your brand and reduce the quality of your work. Instead, continue to refine your expertise in your niche while gradually expanding into related services.

3. **Client Retention and Quality Control** Growth should never come at the cost of your client relationships. As you take on more projects or clients, establish a system for quality control and feedback. Regularly check in with clients to ensure their needs are being met and that they're satisfied with the work. Building long-term relationships with clients can help stabilize your business as you grow.

Hiring and Managing a Remote Team

As a solopreneur, you've likely handled all aspects of your business yourself. However, scaling often requires bringing additional people on board to share the workload. Hiring and managing a remote team is different from managing in-person staff, but with the right approach, it can be incredibly effective.

1. **Outsourcing vs. Hiring Employees**
   One of the first decisions you'll need to make when scaling is whether to hire freelancers or full-time employees. Freelancers are great for specific, project-based work, while full-time employees can help you scale consistently across different areas of your business.

Outsourcing Benefits:

   o Flexible workforce: Freelancers or contractors can be hired on a per-project basis, providing you with flexibility in scaling up or down as needed.

- o Access to specialized skills: You can hire experts for specific tasks like design, marketing, or IT, without committing to full-time salaries.

Hiring Full-Time Employees:

- o Dedicated team: Full-time employees are fully invested in your business and can handle ongoing responsibilities.

- o Team building: A cohesive team can build loyalty, internal culture, and deeper client relationships over time.

2. **Hiring Virtual Assistants** Virtual assistants (VAs) can help with a wide range of administrative and

operational tasks, from managing your calendar to handling customer support and email inquiries. By delegating routine tasks to a VA, you free up time to focus on higher-value activities like client acquisition, strategy, and leadership.

Where to find VAs:

- o Platforms like **Upwork**, **Fiverr**, and **Time Etc** allow you to find and hire skilled virtual assistants.

- o Look for VAs with experience in your industry and a proven track record of reliability and efficiency.

3. **Managing a Remote Team** Managing remote employees or contractors requires clear communication, accountability, and a well-defined workflow. Here are

some key strategies to effectively manage your remote team:

- o **Set Clear Expectations**: From the outset, communicate your expectations regarding deadlines, quality of work, and communication. Establishing these guidelines helps your team deliver results that meet your standards.

- o **Regular Check-Ins**: Schedule regular video or voice meetings to stay updated on progress and address any issues. Tools like Zoom, Slack, or Microsoft Teams make it easy to stay connected.

- o **Use Collaborative Tools**: Implement tools like Trello or Asana for task management and collaboration. These platforms allow your team to stay organized, track progress, and communicate efficiently.

- ○ **Offer Feedback and Recognition**: Regular feedback helps your team members improve and grow, while recognition for a job well done fosters motivation and loyalty.

The Role of Automation in Scaling Your Work-from-Home Business

Automation plays a crucial role in scaling your business by reducing the time spent on repetitive tasks, streamlining workflows, and increasing efficiency. By automating parts of your business, you can focus more on high-impact activities like business development and client relationships.

1. **Automating Administrative Tasks** Administrative work can be time-

consuming, but many aspects of it can be automated. For example:

- o **Email Automation**: Use tools like **Mailchimp** or **ConvertKit** to automate email marketing campaigns, follow-ups, and newsletters.

- o **Invoicing and Accounting**: Tools like **FreshBooks** or **QuickBooks** allow you to automate invoicing, track expenses, and manage payments effortlessly.

- o **Scheduling and Appointments**: Platforms like **Calendly** or **Acuity Scheduling** let clients book meetings with you directly, syncing with your calendar and eliminating back-and-forth communication.

2. **Customer Relationship Management (CRM) Systems** CRM systems like **HubSpot**, **Salesforce**, or **Zoho CRM** allow you to manage customer interactions, track leads, and automate follow-ups. These platforms help you stay on top of your sales pipeline and ensure that no client inquiries fall through the cracks.

3. **Automating Content and Social Media** Content marketing and social media are important components of a growing business, but they can be time-consuming. Tools like **Buffer**, **Hootsuite**, or **Later** allow you to schedule posts across multiple platforms in advance, freeing up time for more strategic activities. Additionally, content automation tools like **CoSchedule** can help plan and execute marketing campaigns efficiently.

Case Studies of Entrepreneurs Who Successfully Scaled

Looking at real-world examples can offer valuable insights into the journey from solo entrepreneur to CEO. Here are two case studies of entrepreneurs who successfully scaled their businesses using remote teams, automation, and outsourcing.

1. **Case Study 1: Brian Clark (Founder of Copyblogger)** Brian Clark started **Copyblogger** as a solo blog in 2006, focusing on copywriting and content marketing advice. By systematizing his approach to content creation and building a community, Clark was able to grow Copyblogger into a full-fledged digital marketing business. He outsourced design, web development, and technical tasks, allowing him to focus on content and business strategy.

Key lessons from Brian Clark:

- Focus on what you do best (in his case, writing and strategy).

- Outsource non-core tasks to experts to maintain quality while scaling.

- Build an engaged community that supports your business growth.

2. **Case Study 2: Nathan Barry (Founder of ConvertKit)** Nathan Barry started **ConvertKit**, an email marketing software, as a solo entrepreneur. Initially, he handled everything from coding to customer support, but as the business grew, he hired a remote team and automated processes like onboarding and customer support. Today, ConvertKit is a multi-million-dollar business with a fully remote team.

Key lessons from Nathan Barry:

- Automate where possible to scale operations efficiently.

- Hire specialists to handle tasks outside your expertise.

- Focus on building a sustainable business model that can grow without your direct involvement in every aspect.

Scaling a remote business from solo operation to a thriving company requires a strategic approach to hiring, automation, and maintaining quality. By systematizing processes, delegating tasks to virtual assistants or a remote team, and leveraging automation tools, you can scale your business while maintaining the high standards that made it successful in the first place. As demonstrated by entrepreneurs like Brian Clark and Nathan Barry, scaling requires smart delegation, the use of technology, and a relentless focus on what truly drives growth. With the right strategies in place, you can transition from a solopreneur to the CEO of a scalable, sustainable business.

Chapter 9: Continuing Education and Skill Development

In the rapidly changing landscape of remote work, staying relevant requires continuous learning and skill development. Whether you're a freelancer, remote employee, or entrepreneur, upskilling is crucial for maintaining a competitive edge and adapting to new industry trends. In this chapter, we'll explore why ongoing education is vital for remote workers, highlight some of the best platforms for learning new skills, and discuss how to network with industry leaders through online communities and webinars to support your professional growth.

Why Continual Education is Vital for Remote Workers

In a world where technology and business practices are evolving at an unprecedented

116

rate, continuous education is not just an option—it's a necessity. As a remote worker, you're expected to be self-reliant and proactive in staying up to date with new skills, tools, and industry trends. Employers and clients increasingly look for individuals who can demonstrate their commitment to lifelong learning and adaptability.

1. **Adapting to New Technologies** Technology is one of the driving forces behind the rise of remote work. As new tools and software become essential to productivity and collaboration, remote workers must be proficient in using them. For example, project management tools like **Trello**, **Asana**, and communication platforms like **Slack** have become integral to remote teams. Learning how to leverage these tools can boost your efficiency

and make you more valuable in the eyes of employers or clients.

2. **Staying Competitive in a Crowded Market** The remote work market has become highly competitive. Whether you are a freelancer, consultant, or remote employee, your skills are your most valuable asset. To stand out from the crowd, you need to continually improve your abilities and knowledge in your niche. Continual education allows you to stay ahead of trends, improve your service offerings, and command higher rates or salaries.

3. **Enhancing Career Flexibility** The more skills you acquire, the more flexible you become in your career path. For example, if you're a content writer, learning SEO, social media marketing, or email marketing can open new avenues for revenue and job opportunities. Flexibility is

crucial for long-term career success, especially in a remote work environment where industry demands can shift quickly.

4. **Navigating Industry Disruptions**
The global workforce is experiencing continuous disruptions—whether through advances in artificial intelligence, automation, or economic shifts. By keeping your skills sharp, you can remain agile and pivot in response to these changes. In fact, many professionals have survived job disruptions by upskilling in areas like digital marketing, coding, or data analysis, making themselves indispensable.

Best Platforms for Learning New Skills

The internet offers an abundance of resources for learning new skills, many of which are tailored for remote workers or those looking to upskill while managing flexible schedules. Below are some of the most highly regarded platforms for continuing education.

1. **Coursera Coursera** partners with universities and organizations worldwide to offer a wide range of courses, specializations, and degrees. With subjects ranging from business and technology to personal development, Coursera is ideal for remote workers looking to gain certifications from reputable institutions like Stanford, Yale, and Google.

   o **Why it's great**: Offers flexible learning options and allows you to earn certificates or even full degrees. Courses often include a mix of video lectures, assignments, and peer-reviewed work, making it engaging and comprehensive.

- **Popular courses**: Data Science, Digital Marketing, and Project Management.

2. **Udemy Udemy** is one of the largest online learning platforms, with over 200,000 courses covering virtually every subject imaginable. Courses are taught by industry professionals and can be completed at your own pace, making it perfect for remote workers with irregular schedules.

   - **Why it's great**: Affordable pricing with frequent discounts and a vast range of courses, from beginner to advanced levels. Many courses offer lifetime access, allowing you to return to the material whenever needed.

   - **Popular courses**: Python for Data Science, Digital

Marketing, Web Development, and Adobe Photoshop.

3. **LinkedIn Learning** **LinkedIn Learning** provides access to thousands of courses in business, technology, and creative fields. It is particularly valuable for professionals looking to enhance skills related to their career path. It also integrates with LinkedIn, allowing you to showcase certifications and completed courses directly on your profile, making you more visible to potential clients or employers.

   o **Why it's great**: Courses are taught by experts and are designed for professional development..

   o **Popular courses**: Leadership, Time Management, and Data Visualization.

4. **Skillshare Skillshare** focuses on creativity, entrepreneurship, and design, offering classes in topics like graphic design, video editing, and writing. It's a fantastic platform for creative professionals who want to learn hands-on skills and build projects along the way.

   o **Why it's great**: Focused on creative and practical skills with project-based learning. You can learn from industry leaders and participate in class projects that help reinforce what you learn.

   o **Popular courses**: Adobe Premiere Pro, Illustration, and Branding for Entrepreneurs.

5. **edX edX** offers courses from top universities such as MIT, Harvard, and Berkeley. Like Coursera, it's ideal for those looking to deepen

their academic knowledge in fields such as data science, computer science, business, and engineering. Many courses are free, and you can pay to receive certifications.

- o **Why it's great**: Access to high-quality education from prestigious institutions. edX also offers MicroMasters programs, which provide graduate-level coursework at a fraction of the cost of traditional programs.

- o **Popular courses**: Artificial Intelligence, Data Science, and Financial Analysis.

Networking with Industry Leaders Through Online Communities and Webinars

While continuous education is essential for skill development, networking with industry professionals and thought leaders is equally important for career growth. Fortunately, there are many online communities and webinars that provide opportunities to connect with experts, learn from their experiences, and expand your professional network.

1. **Online Communities and Forums** Joining online communities in your field can offer invaluable insights and connections. These platforms allow you to engage with peers, share knowledge, and ask for advice. Some popular online communities for remote workers and professionals include:

   o **Reddit**: Subreddits like r/freelance or r/remote work offer discussions and tips from others in your industry.

   o **Slack Groups**: Many industries have dedicated Slack communities where professionals exchange ideas, share resources, and collaborate on projects.

- o **LinkedIn Groups**: Industry-specific LinkedIn Groups allow professionals to participate in discussions, attend virtual events, and network with peers.

2. **Webinars and Virtual Conferences**
   Webinars and virtual conferences have become popular mediums for industry leaders to share their expertise. Many of these events are free or low-cost, and they allow you to gain insights into emerging trends, new technologies, and best practices.

   - o **Why webinars are valuable**: They provide the opportunity to learn directly from industry leaders while also networking with other attendees. Many webinars include Q&A sessions where you can ask questions and engage with the speaker.

- ○ **Popular platforms**: **Zoom**, **Webex**, and **GoToWebinar** are widely used for hosting webinars, while platforms like **Hopin** are designed for virtual conferences and larger online events.

3. **Leveraging LinkedIn for Networking** LinkedIn remains one of the most powerful platforms for professional networking. Engage with content from industry leaders, comment on posts, and reach out to individuals who can help you grow professionally. Participating in LinkedIn Groups or following relevant hashtags can also help you stay updated with the latest industry

trends and connect with like-minded professionals.

How to network on LinkedIn:

- o **Engage with posts and articles**: Leave thoughtful comments on posts from industry leaders or peers to build visibility.

- o **Send personalized connection requests**: When reaching out to potential contacts, make sure to personalize your message and explain why you'd like to connect.

- o **Share your knowledge**: Post regularly to showcase your expertise and stay active within your professional network.

In the world of remote work, continual education and skill development are critical to maintaining your competitive edge and adapting to a constantly evolving landscape. With platforms like Coursera, Udemy, and LinkedIn Learning at your fingertips, upskilling has never been more accessible. Combine that with the power of networking through online communities and webinars, and you'll have the tools necessary to stay relevant, grow your career, and succeed in the remote workforce.

Chapter 10: Building a Sustainable Work-Life Balance

Achieving long-term success while working remotely hinges on maintaining a healthy balance between professional responsibilities and personal well-being. While remote work offers flexibility, it can also blur the boundaries between work and life, leading to burnout or neglect of essential aspects like mental health, family, and financial planning. This chapter will provide practical strategies for creating a sustainable work-from-home lifestyle, focusing on work-life balance, financial planning, and mental and physical health.

Maintaining Work-Life Balance in a Remote Setting

Remote work offers unprecedented flexibility, but without clear boundaries, it can lead to overworking or a feeling of always being "on." A sustainable work-life balance involves setting boundaries between work and personal life, developing routines that prioritize both productivity and relaxation, and being mindful of the need for downtime.

1. **Create a Designated Workspace**
   One of the most important aspects of work-life balance is separating your workspace from your living space. Whether it's a home office or a dedicated corner in your home, having a designated workspace signals the start and end of your workday. This physical separation helps create a psychological barrier, reducing the temptation to work during non-work hours.

Tips for setting up a designated workspace:

- Choose a space that's quiet and free from distractions.

- Equip your workspace with the right tools and technology to stay productive.

- Set up your workspace ergonomically to avoid physical strain, which can improve both your comfort and efficiency.

2. **Set Boundaries and Stick to a Routine** Creating a schedule and sticking to it helps maintain structure in your day. Designate specific hours for work and personal time, and try to maintain consistent start and end times for your workday. Establish clear boundaries with colleagues and clients, communicating when you are available and when you are off the clock.

Strategies for effective boundaries:

- Use tools like **Google Calendar** or **TimeCamp** to block off time for both work and personal activities.

- Set limits on responding to work emails or messages outside of your designated working hours.

- Take regular breaks throughout the day, such as following the **Pomodoro Technique** or scheduling lunchtime walks.

3. **Develop a Wind-Down Routine** To disconnect from work, develop a wind-down routine that signals the end of your workday. This could be shutting down your computer, doing a few stretches, or going for a short walk. Having a routine helps you transition mentally from work mode

to relaxation, which is essential for work-life balance.

Wind-down routine ideas:

- o Close out work-related apps or tabs on your computer.
- o Take five minutes to tidy up your workspace.
- o Engage in a calming activity like reading, yoga, or light exercise.

Financial Planning for Long-Term Success

Sustainable long-term success in a remote work lifestyle also depends on financial planning. Remote workers often deal with irregular income streams or self-employment, which can complicate saving and investing. Establishing a solid financial plan can provide peace of mind and set you up for long-term stability.

1. **Create an Emergency Fund**
Whether you're a freelancer or employed remotely, having an emergency fund is crucial for managing unpredictable expenses. A general rule of thumb is to save three to six months' worth of living expenses. This fund can be used for unforeseen circumstances, such as losing a client or unexpected health issues.

Steps to build an emergency fund:

- o Set up automatic transfers to a high-yield savings account.

- o Start small by contributing a percentage of each paycheck or freelance payment.

- o Prioritize consistency over the amount—small, regular contributions can accumulate over time.

2. **Retirement Planning for Remote Workers** Many remote workers or freelancers do not have access to traditional employer-sponsored retirement plans. It's essential to take charge of your own retirement savings by contributing to an Individual Retirement Account (IRA) or other retirement vehicles like a Solo 401(k).

Retirement saving tips:

- Contribute to a **Roth IRA** or **Traditional IRA**. Depending on your income and tax strategy, you can choose between tax-free withdrawals or tax-deductible contributions.

- If you're self-employed, explore **Solo 401(k)** options, which allow you to save more annually than a traditional IRA.

- o Automate contributions so that a portion of your income goes directly into retirement savings.

3. **Diversify Income Streams** To ensure long-term financial growth, consider diversifying your income streams. As discussed in **Chapter 5**, building multiple revenue streams through passive income, side gigs, or investments helps protect you against fluctuations in your primary income.

Ways to diversify income:

- o Invest in the stock market through platforms like **Robinhood** or **Acorns** to grow your wealth over time.

- Build passive income streams by selling digital products, e-books, or online courses.

- Offer consulting or coaching services in your area of expertise to diversify your client base.

Mental and Physical Health Strategies for Remote Workers

Working remotely often presents unique challenges to both mental and physical health. Without the natural boundaries of an office environment, it's easy to neglect self-care or experience burnout. Prioritizing both mental and physical well-being is essential for long-term success.

1. **Prioritize Physical Health** Sitting for long periods of time in front of a computer can lead to physical discomfort or long-term health problems. Incorporating movement into your daily routine, practicing

good posture, and taking care of your body will help maintain your health as a remote worker.

Physical health tips:

- o Set a timer to stand up and stretch every 30 minutes.

- o Consider a sit-stand desk to alternate between sitting and standing during the day.

- o Incorporate at-home workouts, such as bodyweight exercises, yoga, or resistance training, into your routine to stay active.

2. **Protect Your Mental Health** Remote workers can sometimes experience feelings of isolation, stress, or burnout due to the lack of social interaction and increased pressure to stay productive. Establishing routines that prioritize

mental health is crucial for maintaining balance.

Strategies for mental well-being:

- o Take mental health breaks throughout the day, such as practicing mindfulness or meditation.

- o Schedule regular check-ins with friends, family, or colleagues to stay connected socially.

- o Set realistic expectations for your work output and avoid overloading your schedule.

3. **Maintain a Healthy Work-Life Balance** Achieving work-life balance is an ongoing process, especially when working from home. Regularly evaluate how much time you're dedicating to work versus personal activities. Ensure that you're setting

aside time for hobbies, relaxation, and family.

Work-life balance strategies:

- o Schedule personal activities, such as family dinners, movie nights, or outdoor activities, into your calendar.

- o Avoid using work devices or checking emails during your personal time.

- o Pursue hobbies and creative outlets to unwind and detach from work stress.

Achieving long-term success in remote work is not just about managing tasks and projects—it's about building a sustainable lifestyle that supports your mental, physical, and financial well-being. By maintaining work-life boundaries, developing strong financial habits, and prioritizing health, remote workers can thrive both professionally and personally. With the right strategies in place, you can enjoy the freedom and flexibility of remote work while securing a stable future for yourself and your loved ones.

Conclusion

As the world continues to embrace remote work, the ability to adapt, learn, and thrive in a home-based work environment becomes increasingly essential. Throughout this book, we've explored the key elements necessary for success in a remote work setting—ranging from building a productive work environment and managing your time effectively to scaling your business and maintaining a balanced, fulfilling life.

The journey to mastering remote work is not a one-size-fits-all approach. Every individual's path will vary, but the core principles of ongoing education, work-life balance, and smart financial planning will remain universal. Whether you are starting your journey as a freelancer, entrepreneur, or remote employee, or you are looking to scale and evolve your career further, the strategies outlined in this book will help guide you towards long-term success.

Key Takeaways:

- **Time Management and Productivity:** Learning to manage your time through techniques like the Pomodoro Technique and utilizing tools like Trello and Asana is critical for remote success.

- **Scaling and Outsourcing:** As your business grows, leveraging automation, outsourcing tasks, and building a remote team will help you scale without losing quality.

- **Lifelong Learning:** Continuous education through platforms like Coursera, Udemy, and LinkedIn Learning is essential for staying competitive and relevant in the fast-evolving digital landscape.

- **Work-Life Balance:** Ensuring a healthy balance between professional duties and personal life, while prioritizing mental and physical health, is key to avoiding burnout and maintaining long-term sustainability.

- **Financial Planning:** Planning for long-term financial security through smart budgeting, emergency funds, and diversified income streams will ensure you thrive in the remote work lifestyle.

By applying the insights, tools, and strategies in this book, you can create a remote work life that not only supports your career goals but also fosters a sense of fulfillment and well-being. Remember that the remote work journey is a marathon, not a sprint. Success comes from consistent effort, a willingness to adapt, and a commitment to personal and professional growth.

Here's to your continued success in the remote work revolution!

References

1. **Ferriss, Timothy**. *The 4-Hour Workweek: Escape 9-5, Live Anywhere, and Join the New Rich*. Crown Publishing, 2007.

    o   A foundational resource on time management, outsourcing, and creating multiple streams of passive income.

2. **Newport, Cal**. *Deep Work: Rules for Focused Success in a Distracted World*. Grand Central Publishing, 2016.

    o   A guide to mastering focus and productivity, especially relevant for remote workers who must manage distractions at home.

3. **Clark, Brian**. *Copyblogger*. Available at: https://copyblogger.com

- A rich resource for freelancers and entrepreneurs on how to build an online presence, scale businesses, and develop content marketing strategies.

4. **Barry, Nathan**. *Authority: A Step-By-Step Guide to Self-Publishing*. ConvertKit, 2014.

- Discusses the transition from freelancer to business owner, scaling digital products, and building passive income streams.

Online Learning Platforms:

5. **Coursera**. Available at: https://coursera.org

- Offers a wide range of courses on topics such as data science, business, and project management. Particularly helpful for continuous learning and skill development in a remote work context.

6. **Udemy**. Available at: https://udemy.com

    o   Provides affordable online courses on numerous topics, from programming to digital marketing, perfect for upskilling in various remote work niches.

7. **LinkedIn Learning**. Available at: https://linkedin.com/learning

    o   A comprehensive platform for professional development, featuring courses on leadership, time management, and scaling businesses.

Tools and Resources:

8. **Trello**. Available at: https://trello.com

- A project management tool that allows users to organize tasks visually, which is crucial for remote workers managing multiple projects.

9. **Asana**. Available at: https://asana.com

- A task management tool that helps remote teams collaborate and manage projects more efficiently.

10. **Slack**. Available at: https://slack.com

- A collaboration platform for remote teams, used to enhance communication and streamline workflows.

Financial Planning Resources:

11. **FreshBooks**. Available at: https://freshbooks.com

- An accounting software designed for freelancers and small businesses, perfect for managing finances as a remote worker.

12. **Solo 401(k) for Self-Employed**. IRS.gov. Available at: https://www.irs.gov/retirement-plans/one-participant-401k-plans

- Information about retirement planning options for freelancers and entrepreneurs.

13. **Investopedia**. *How to Build an Emergency Fund*. Available at: https://www.investopedia.com/articles/pf/06/emergencyfund.asp

- A practical guide to building an emergency fund, which is crucial for financial security in a remote work lifestyle.

About the Author

Evelyn Carter is a prolific writer, speaker, and entrepreneur, known for her insightful work on personal development and remote work strategies. She has authored several best-selling books on business, productivity, and mental health, including *"Mastering the Remote Life: How to Thrive as a Digital Nomad"* and *"The Balanced Entrepreneur: Strategies for Long-Term Success in the Digital Age."*

Born in 1982 in Austin, Texas, Evelyn grew up in a family of entrepreneurs. Her parents ran a small but successful organic farming business, where she developed an early interest in business strategy and innovation. She pursued a degree in **Business Administration** from the University of Texas, where she also discovered her passion for writing and teaching others about personal growth.

Evelyn began her career in corporate consulting, working with Fortune 500 companies to improve their internal communication systems and remote work policies. However, after several years in the corporate world, she realized her true passion was helping individuals unlock their potential through remote work and entrepreneurship. In 2010, she left the corporate world to pursue a freelance career, eventually building her own online consulting firm focused on helping freelancers and small business owners scale their businesses.

Her groundbreaking first book, *"Mastering the Remote Life,"* was published in 2015 and quickly became a go-to resource for remote workers seeking practical advice on balancing productivity and mental well-being. Since then, Evelyn has expanded her influence by hosting online courses and webinars on platforms like Udemy and LinkedIn Learning, where she shares her expertise in digital marketing, leadership, and time management.

Carter is known for her engaging speaking style and has been invited to speak at events like the **Global Remote Work Summit** and the **Entrepreneurship World Forum**. Her thought leadership in remote work has earned her features in publications like **Forbes**, **Inc. Magazine**, and **The Remote Work Journal**.

In addition to her professional work, Evelyn is an advocate for mental health awareness, particularly for remote workers who face the challenges of isolation and burnout. She regularly contributes to **Mindful Work**, a blog dedicated to mental wellness in the modern workplace.

Evelyn lives in Portland, Oregon, with her husband and two children. When she isn't writing or coaching entrepreneurs, she enjoys hiking, experimenting with sustainable farming techniques in her backyard, and traveling to remote locations for inspiration.

Disclaimer

The information presented in this book is for educational and informational purposes only and is not intended as legal, financial, medical, or professional advice. While the author has made every effort to ensure the accuracy and completeness of the information provided, the reader is encouraged to consult with appropriate professionals before making any decisions based on the content of this book.

The author and publisher shall not be held liable for any loss or damage resulting from the use of the information contained herein. The strategies and examples discussed are based on personal experiences and research, and results may vary depending on individual circumstances.

Additionally, this book may contain references to third-party products, services, or websites. These references are provided for the convenience of the reader and do not constitute an endorsement or recommendation by the author or publisher. The author and publisher do not assume any responsibility for the accuracy or availability of the information provided by these third-party sources.

Copyright